Oldham
Council

D0270639

LEES		
15/3/16		

Please return this book before the last date stamped.
Items can be renewed by telephone, in person at any library or online at
www.oldham.gov.uk/libraries

The
SICK BAG
Song

Nick Cave

CANONGATE
Edinburgh · London

This paperback edition published by Canongate Books in 2016
14 High Street, Edinburgh EH1 1TE

www.canongate.tv

1

Designed by Pentagram

ISBN 978 1 78211 793 3

Printed and bound in Great Britain by Clays Ltd, St Ives plc

To the boy on the bridge

Nashville
Tennessee

A young boy climbs a riverbank. He steps onto a railway bridge. He is twelve years old.

He kneels down, under a harsh sun, and puts his ear to the track. The track does not vibrate. There is no train approaching around the bend on the other side of the river.

The boy starts to run along the tracks. He arrives in the middle of the bridge. He stands on the edge and looks down at the muddy river below.

On the left side is a concrete pylon that supports the bridge. On the right, a half-felled tree lies across the river, its branches sticking out into the dark water. In between there is a small space about four feet wide.

He has been told that it is possible to jump in at this point, but he cannot be sure, as he has never seen anybody do it.

The stones beneath his feet begin to tremble. He crouches down and again he puts his ear to the track.

The track begins to vibrate. The train is coming.

He stares down at the dark, muddy water, his heart pounding.

•

The boy does not realise that he is not a boy at all, but rather the memory of a boy.

He is the memory of a boy running through the mind of a man in a suite at the Sheraton Hotel in downtown Nashville, Tennessee, who is being injected in the thigh with a steroid shot that will transform the jet-lagged, flu-ridden singer into a deity.

In three hours he will burst from the hotel room. He will move through the empty city, crossing vast rivers, driving through empty prairies, along tremendous, multi-laned highways, under darkening skies, like a small god, to be with you, tonight.

Manchester
Tennessee

And I will walk on stage at Bonnaroo Festival in Manchester, Tennessee, and become an object of great fascination to almost no one. The dazed crowd will drift back and forth across the fields and the sinking sun will flood the site with orange fire. After the show, I will sit outside on the steps of our trailer and smoke.

On the way back to Nashville, our van will be stalled on the highway for two hours at the scene of a terrible automobile accident. We will watch as ambulances and police cars speed down the slip roads. We will see a helicopter chopping above us, its searchlight cutting through the dark night. For an hour we will sit silently in our van, smoking and drinking. Eventually our tour manager will leave the vehicle to investigate. He will come back to report that two vehicles have collided, up ahead, and a girl lies decapitated on the road.

I will fall asleep in the back of the van, waking up when our vehicle begins to move. From the slow-moving side window I will see the decapitated body lying on the road, covered by a grim, bulging, blue plastic sheet.

I will pick at a thread in my jacket sleeve all the way back to the Sheraton in downtown Nashville. Pick, pick, pick.

An angel will unfold its wings and speak into my ear.

You must take the first step alone.

Then the angel will nudge me and send me sailing out into the unknown.

This is how I will begin The Sick Bag Song.

Louisville
Kentucky

You must take the first step alone.
I move tentatively toward the lip of the world.
North America stretches out before me like a split bag of sick.
The nine daughter-Muses sweeten their encouraging breath.
And the nine unfolding angels prepare to bear me away.

Bear me away on their white wings to Louisville, Kentucky,
Where I walk across the Big Four Pedestrian and Bicycle Bridge,
Eating fried chicken, right across the mighty Ohio. *Right on!*

And leaning against the railing, staring down at the water below,
I see a black girl in a tiny stars-and-stripes mini-skirt.
I open up my sick bag and say, *Right on! Jump in!* By the way,
This is exactly the sort of thing that will end up getting me hurt.

The girl in the stars-and-stripes mini-skirt leans out.
She elicits the sympathy of the entire world by revealing
The touching forethought of a sudden matching thong.

I am going to put that in my sick bag song!
I don't care about the flak!
I've got a flak jacket with the stars and stripes on!

The jacket is actually a sick bag,
And the sick bag is a long, slow-motion love song,

That has something to do with the ballad of 'The Butcher Boy',
Which ends with the line – *That the world may know I died of love.*

The girl places a single, shoeless foot on the railing of the bridge.
And then stands up on the barrier.

Take care, I say, and the girl turns to me and smiles and salutes.

My wife once heard 'The Butcher Boy' sung so beautifully she cried.
She folded up her flak jacket, closed her eyes and basically died.

I am a small god made of terracotta, trembling on a pedestal,
Interred in a maelstrom of sound.

Look what the little clay god has found, neatly folded!
A jumbled bundle of young black bones,
Secured by a teeny half-digested thong.

I read somewhere that my best work was behind me.
But where? When I turn around, the flying girl is gone.

•

The next morning, I stand in the lobby of the 21c Museum
Hotel in Louisville, awed by four terracotta sculptures of naked
children, by the artist Judy Fox, arranged in a row behind
the reception desk. They are really something to see as you
check out of your hotel. The little child-heroes are small,
scorched gods. They press their young faces against the
windows of the iconic roles they are set to play. Look at
them on their shuddering pedestals! Look at them standing
on the precipice of their child-selves, with their baked and
bletting bodies, preparing to leap! Look at them!

•

Later still, we file onto the bus and our tour manager counts
heads and we cling to our paper coffee cups, and as the bus
turns into Main Street down comes a sudden summer shower
and someone puts on 'Kentucky Rain' by Elvis Presley and I see,
through the window, for an instant, along one of the adjacent
streets that leads to the Ohio River, under the Big Four
Pedestrian and Bicycle Bridge, a group of representatives from
the emergency services, dressed in black jackets and peaked
caps, dragging something from the rain-pocked river.

Kansas City
Missouri

I am a nervous system that runs on rhyme and ghosts.
The ghosts howl through the words making them chime.
I'd no idea I may have tasted your sweet breath
For the last time,
And when I think of you at home I notice
A brief expansion of worried longing in my chest,
As we cross the state line into Missouri,
And park our bus by the side of the road and disembark,
And in the unhurried dark, enter the low grass of the prairie
On our bellies like snakes.

We enact the slaughter of the bison by William 'Buffalo Bill' Cody,
Then the Indian Wars including the Battle of Coon Creek.
And that night at the Intercontinental in Kansas City,
I try to call you on the transatlantic communications cable,
But the phone just rings and rhymes.
So I leave an obscure, disembodied message
On our answering machine. It goes –

> *You are the statuesque bison standing in the prairie of my leave.*
> *You are Squanto's grief upon returning home.*
> *You are the tear spilt on the rawhide sleeve.*
> *Pick up the phone*
> *Pick up the phone*
> *I am the skinned hump that paints the prairie red.*
> *I am the guy with the flies. I am the one that dies.*
> *I am the man that goes on tour and hides.*
> *I am the one that wed and fled.*
> *Pick up the phone*
> *Pick up the phone*
> *I am the dead.*

Then I take a pill and go to bed.

•

Under the bed sheet, I place the sick bag to my ear and shake it. I hear the rattle of the nine Muses' emblems – the writing tablet, the scroll, the flute, the arrows of love, the tragic mask, the harp, the lyre, the comic mask, the globe and compass.

I can hear the warm blood seeping onto the highway, from my severed neck, as I phone home and you do not answer.

I can hear the young boy's terrible heart calibrating itself to the train that is rushing towards him.

I hear bloodless people, whispering, commiserating and plotting. I recognise these voices as collaborators from a distant past.

My nine naked Muses sleep softly, piled on my chest, for their work is done for today.

I regulate my breathing as the unfolding angels wing me away.

In sleep, I am borne across a gentle, purple North American dreamscape – a panorama of solution and resolution, where the next action that is best for us is effortlessly revealed.

Milwaukee
Wisconsin

Then in the morning we bus it up to Milwaukee,
Where if you are not German then you're a Pole.
At least that's what the guy from Mader's Restaurant says,
As he serves us a pretzel big as a severed human head.

Then into the rainy night we run, to the Intercontinental Hotel,
Our blue plastic flak jackets pulled over our heads,
Past the autograph hounds and into the bathroom mirror, I sing,

When I wear this mask the girls all scream
When I wear this one they laugh instead.
When I hit Milwaukee with a pint of cream,
They pull the sheets over their heads.

I carefully concoct a paste in a bowl and I paint my hair black,
So that it sits like a sleek, inky raven's wing
On top of my multi-storey forehead. I lean in and gaze deep
Into the confused crop-circles of my eyes. In the right eye,
In the blue, is a little brown discolouration and the whites
Are beginning to yellow. There is a liver spot on my left temple.
A spider-vein on my right nostril. The bathroom light is brutal.
I reposition my face so that I stop looking
Like Kim Jong-un and start looking more like Johnny Cash,
Or someone. Hang on! Just a minute! There you go! Like that!

•

In a studio in Malibu, Johnny Cash sat down and played a song.
He was partially blind and could barely walk. I was there.
I saw a sick man pick up his instrument and be well.
With regret I have seen the opposite too. Pick, pick, pick.
I have seen well men pick up their instruments and be sick.

•

Resist the urge to create.
Resist the belief in the absurd.
Resist by means of provocation.
Resist by means of sickness and sadness.
Resist by means of masturbation.
Resist by motivational manuals.
Resist by doing for others.
Resist by comparison to others.
Resist through the opinions of others.

These are *The Nine Bedevilments of Advancement*. They live in our
blood and skin and nerves. They are as present and cataclysmic
to our progress as a runaway train thundering towards us, as we
stand rigid with fear on the tracks.

The oozing entrails of my sick bag sweep stars and stripes
Across the sawdust floor of the USA. But, *hark!*
What is that sweet breath behind my ear, I hear you say?
It is the Muses and Johnny Cash blowing us along our way.

Minneapolis
Minnesota

I am vomiting up Milwaukee's mussels and pretzel in an alley
Behind the State Theatre in Minneapolis, Minnesota.
Minneapolis with its sensible weatherproof walkways,
And the State Theatre in the free Italian Renaissance style,
Its restored proscenium curving a hundred feet above the stage,
Bought by Live Nation in the year two thousand,
Then sold to Key Entertainment in two thousand and eight.
We arrive early but we get sick and we go on late.
The show of warmth from the crowd is staggering. *Look!*
The audience are turning their bodies into concrete pylons!
Their arms reach out like the lethal branches of half-felled trees!
The music rumbles towards us along the tracks!
We have waded through the blood of buffalo
And Cheyenne warriors to be with you tonight. *Look!*
The concrete pylons are turning into columns of light.
I stand like a flayed dog on my hind legs and reveal
An extending stripe of wet, pink skin. *Leap!* I say,
Fumbling with my doggie bag of sick. *Leap, you fuckers!*
And all the columns of light hold hands and, one by one, jump in.

•

That late night in the Grand Hotel in downtown Minneapolis
I approach John Berryman's *Dream Songs*
Like a master thief. I slow my heartbeat,
And press my ear up the eighteen rails
Of dark, vibrating verse. My innards rumble like a train.
Slowly, patiently the tumblers click and with terror
And comfort the entire world falls out. I yawn.

Then I dream on down to Washington Avenue Bridge,
Where the poet debated the subtle difference between
Flying and falling with the pretty lawny bank below.
You must take the first step alone –
A fraudster angel with paper wings tied to its back, like a sail
Said, You must take the first step alone! *And, so too, the last!*
Then he kicked John Berryman over the rail.

And as the concertinaed poet suffocated on the grass,
I hit the fourth line of 'Dream Song 54' like a runaway train
'I prop on the costly bed & think of my wife'
And awaken with a rush and a shrieking need,
And dial, dial, dial, my wife! *Don't jump! My God!*
My pretty baby, don't jump! Pick up the phone!
As I remember, on the goodbye steps of our house,
Her wet, unstable eye, that said, *huh, huh, huh,*
Don't leave. Don't go. Stay home.

•

The Sick Bag Song is the leavings.
The Sick Bag Song is the scrapings.
The Sick Bag Song is the shavings.
The Sick Bag Song is the last vestiges.
The Sick Bag Song is the bile and the tripe.
The Sick Bag Song is the remnants and the residue.
The Sick Bag Song is the leftovers and the throwbacks.
The Sick Bag Song is the barrel's dreggy bottom.
The Sick Bag Song is the rejectamenta, disgorged –

So that we can move forward and tomorrow leap differently.

Denver
Colorado

We flew to Denver from Minneapolis on United. *Right on!*
Grabbed some sick bags so I'd have something to write on!

•

In Denver I buy a lovely little book by Patti Smith called
Woolgathering and she writes about having possessed a kind
of *knapsack* full of souvenirs – a ruby, a spoon, the insides of
a walkie-talkie. It's a lovely thing to read under a blue sky on a
bench in Colfax Street in Denver. *Right on, Patti!*

I pick her up by her braids and drop her into my sick bag.

I look inside.

I can see a tiny Gertrude Stein and a little Emily Dickinson.
I can see a miniature Philip Larkin pushing a lawnmower,
and a little wrinkly W. H. Auden. I can see a pygmy dressed
as John Berryman with a bone through his nose and loads
of other people too. A small-scale late-period Elvis, a tiny
John Lee Hooker with stars-and-stripes socks, a crazy little
James Brown and a bent-backed Hank Williams in a Resistol
Rancher hat.

These are the lollipop ladies, with their severed heads on pikes,
shepherding me across these lost and lonely highways and into
your arms tonight.

And in a dark, dejected corner of my sick bag sits a tiny Bryan
Ferry in a pair of blue swimming trunks, in West Sussex, in the
summer of 2000.

•

The stretched sky was blue and so hot my wife was sick with it. She was eight months pregnant with the twins, swollen and gasping for air, unrecognisable from the willowy woman I married a year ago. She stepped out of the car, a beautiful elephant of woe, stepped out and onto Bryan Ferry's driveway.

My wife and I had come to visit Lucy Ferry. Bryan was away on business. I was relieved. Who wants to meet their childhood heroes?

Lucy showed us around the grounds. We saw the walled garden all in bloom, we saw the orchard full of apples, we saw the swallows and the martins, we saw the foaling horse prancing in the fields.

In the noonday sun the women were as white as snowflakes. I drifted away and found a swimming pool surrounded by a high hedge. I took off my jacket and sat down on a lounger under an umbrella and fell asleep.

I awoke to find Bryan Ferry in his bathers, standing in the swimming pool. He was white and handsome and very still.

I haven't written a song in three years, he said.

Why? What's wrong with you? I said.

He gestured, with an uncertain hand, all about him.

There is nothing to write about, he said.

Then he pushed off into the water.

That night I sat at my desk writing in a frenzy – page upon page – song after song – I couldn't stop! But weeping too! Hot, sobbing tears pouring down my cheeks.

Hey, what's the matter, baby? said my wife, propped up on the bed.

I'm a fucking vampire! I cried, thinking of Bryan Ferry and his bursting flowers and his prancing horses and his flight of swallows and his hedged swimming pool and his lovely wife.

No, you're not. Come here, she said.

I crawled onto the bed and she pulled the sheet away.

Listen, she said.

I put my ear against her distended stomach, her *knapsack*, and listened. I could hear little trapped people swimming around within.

They are eating me from the inside, she said.

Lucky them, I said.

I'm serious, she said.

But she had fallen asleep and I crawled off the bed across the floor, up the wainscot and along the panelled ceiling. I pressed my ear to the ceiling and listened. I could hear people gathering on the floor above. The ceiling vibrated. I recognised the voices as past collaborators, going back many years. They sounded fatigued as if depleted of oxygen, maybe, or as if someone had siphoned their blood away. I could hear them sobbing and cursing and consoling each other.

I fell asleep.

Calgary
Alberta

I awake hanging from the ceiling fan in the Westin, Calgary, Southern Alberta. I spider down into my clothes and fling wide the window!

Blue skies, motherfucker! Day off!

Everything we do is for a better you! says the mission statement on the lobby wall as I high-five the doorman and hit the street at a cheerful pace.

O lovely Calgary, Alberta! What a bright and pretty spot!

I cross the pleasant Bow River under a faultless sky and stroll along the Chevron Learning Pathway – the fabulous environmental educational walkway on the east end of Prince's Island Park. I wind my way through a constructed wetland, and by a clump of purple blazing star, a family of dabbling ducks waddles by, followed by a solitary stinger bee and up above, a white bell-shaped cloud floats across the sky and suddenly and out of nowhere, a feeling hits me like a kick in the guts, *huh, huh, huh*, for it suddenly grows dark, so I hurry back to the hotel, black smoke in my chest, and write a song until *huh, huh, huh*, half past fucking three. It went –

I was born in a puddle of blood wanting everything.
The blood was my own, pumping from my infant heart.
I weighed myself and found myself wanting, wanting everything.
Wanting everything is the thing that eventually tears you apart.

I spend my days pushing Elvis Presley's belly up a series of steep hills.
Wanting everything is the everything that eventually kills.
In the morning I attach my king-sized shadow to my heels.
Without my shadow I don't know how the other half feels.

I'm standing in the dressing room with a mushroom cloud for a head.
My cock sticks out like a sore thumb. I long for my hotel bed.
I say, I wonder who I have to blow around here to get ahead?
Wanting everything is the everything that eventually kills you dead.

These king-sized tears do not come from me but beyond me,
Drowning my eyes with floods of unexpected memory,
Of a time of wanting, wanting it all, wanting everything.
Stop now! Let it go! You are completely enough!

And called it 'King-Sized Nick Cave Blues' and climbed into bed,
and thumbing through the Gideon's Bible — 1 Samuel 7 — I read,

Then David took his staff in his hand, chose a number of smooth
stones from the stream, put each of them in his nine shepherd's bags,
his pouches —

The elegant Air Canada sick bag,
The efficient American Airlines sick bag,
The grim, grey British Airways sick bag,
The functional Alaska Airlines sick bag,
The instructional Delta Air Lines sick bag,
The hip, extroverted Virgin Atlantic sick bag,
The exploitative Qantas airline sick bag,
The boring Southwest Airlines 'advertisement' sick bag,
The useless, ink-resistant plastic-coated United Airlines sick
bag,

and with his sling in his hand, David approached the Philistine.

So David triumphed over the Philistine with a sling and a stone. Without
a sword in his hand he struck down the Philistine and killed him. Wham!
Right between the fucking eyes! David ran and stood over him. He took
hold of the Philistine's sword and drew it from the sheath. He cut off his
head with the sword.

•

I like 'King-Sized Nick Cave Blues'. I think it has a lot going for it. I like the idea of our longings ultimately destroying us – it's weirdly comforting, even though it's not really true. It's our *lack of longing* that gets us in the end. I am really pleased with the line about my cock sticking out like a sore thumb – you can't buy that shit! – and I like the image of pushing Elvis Presley's belly up a hill – the Sisyphean burden of our influences. As much as we twist and turn, they are never really transcended. They are seared into our souls like a brand. But mostly I like the last unrhymed line that suddenly and abruptly decapitates the song with a command from some less indulgent part of me – to basically stop moaning and shut the fuck up. *Right on!*

•

The next night, the air-conditioning is set to *polar* at the Southern Alberta Jubilee Auditorium, in Calgary. By *polar*, I mean that when I try to enter the band-room, I find that it has frozen solid, a great block of barely transparent ice, and trapped inside, Warren, like a psychedelic Early Man, crouches over his violin and bow, a cake of pine rosin in his hand. In the centre of the iceberg, Marty and Conway face each other, caught in time, each holding an enormous glass of Pinot Noir, with looks of intense concentration on their faces as if attempting to stay balanced on a see-saw. Meanwhile, in a secluded corner, behind massive, gold-rimmed shades, Barry sits, hatless, snap-frozen and unmoving, while George leans, handsomely encased in ice, one hand caught mid-journey toward the sushi platter. Jim, an actual giant, towers above them all, work-busted hands behind his back, angled forwards from the waist, as if weighed down by his spade-shaped beard.

The assistant tour manager shouts through the door *Showtime!* and the ice instantly crumbles and melts away and we move down the hall and into the hellish lights and the suffocating, deoxygenated air. And as we take up our positions on the stage, we call upon the nine Muses for assistance,

Calliope, who helps with the epic ballads,
Euterpe, who helps with the sad songs,
Erato, who helps with the confessional songs,
Clio, who helps with the oldies,
Melpomene, who helps with the super-tragic stuff,
Polyhymnia, who helps with the religious songs,
Terpsichore, who helps with the dance numbers,
Thalia, who helps with the funny songs,
And Urania, who helps when it gets spacey and psychedelic.

The nine Muses wait in the wings and upon hearing our petition, flash their AAA passes and jostle for space with the nine choruses of the angels,

Seraphs, who keep us sexy and freewheeling,
Cherubs, who stop us doing anything too stupid,
Thrones, who keep us strong and virile,
Dominations, who free our minds, *Right on!*
Principalities, who stop us getting weepy and nostalgic,
Powers, who transform us into small gods,
Vertues, who keep us humble,
Archangels, who deal with the cops,
And ordinary angels, who keep us child-like.

We call upon them all, this diverse and squabbling army of inspiration, to each breathe their curling tendrils of transmutation and combustion across the stage, so that we can begin, *in love*, and get this fucking show on the road.

Look! Here they come, these figments of the imagination — invisible, silent, odourless, tasteless! You can't see them, you say? Where are they, you say? Oh, my darlings, they are within us and without us, above us and below us and all about us! Look! Here they come now, with my fucked-up, spade-shaped, sad-sack sick bag song!

Edmonton
Alberta

At the Fairmont Hotel Macdonald in Edmonton, Alberta,
A piece of old Europe hanging from the valley wall,
The only Four Diamond Rated Luxury Hotel in Edmonton.
Mythology bubbled up about me like melted plastic.
But be warned! The Fairmont Hotel's dry-cleaning service,
Basically Chernobyled my suit enough to make me gag,
Which I wore to the Northern Alberta Jubilee Auditorium,
Where Procol Harum recorded *Procol Harum Live In Concert
With The Edmonton Symphony Orchestra* in 1971,
With an awesome version of 'Conquistador', with drumming
By the amazing B. J. Wilson, who was born in Edmonton, England.
How weird is that? Edmonton in Northern Alberta
Was named after Edmonton in England in 1791 as the new
Trading post for the Hudson Bay Company, don't you know.

That night, our work done, we rolled out of the Jubilee,
Down the valley and swam around in the Saskatchewan,
Then partied with some comely Canadian fur traders,
Like it was seventeen ninety-one.

Mythology bubbles up about me like melted plastic.

I sit alone on the bank of the glacial Saskatchewan,
Beside a low-lying bridge,
Picking at a thread in my jacket sleeve. Pick, pick, pick.
Cubic tonnes of water spew along the river's course.

The river is a pulsating, living artery.
It has nine known qualities.

> It is not ashamed of its actions.
> It flows without resistance.
> It washes its own history away.
> It has no memory.
> It is eternally of the present and in the present.
> It is not dependent on the whims of the muse.
> It needs no angels to transport it.

It is not petrified, haunted or derelict.
It is not fumigated.

I strip off my reeking sick bag suit and rinse it in the river. Wash away the Fairmont Hotel Macdonald's dry-cleaning service's toxins all the way to Lake Winnipeg!

And naked, I drift into a sort of reverie.

•

I remember the disastrous events from the town of my youth. The boy who accidentally shot and killed his brother in the street next to ours. The boy who had a fatal allergic reaction to multiple bee stings. The old dead man we found in a gully on the way to school. But mostly I remember what my mother and father told me about the boy who had died jumping off the railway bridge. He had hit the concrete pylon support that lay submerged beneath the water and was knocked unconscious. He drowned. He was found a couple of days later tangled in the branches of the half-felled tree. Mostly I remember that.

I light a cigarette, and resting there on the bank stare out across the dark, moonlit river and wonder how many memories I have mislaid along the way and whether they will ever be retrieved. Without warning, I am overwhelmed by a particular kind of sorrow, swollen and hard in my chest, that is reserved for the loss of something both utterly precious and entirely illusory, and my eyes well with tears that spill down my cheeks.

•

I stay that way for a time, until I become aware of a shallow breathing coming from beneath the bridge. I rise to my feet and, hunching down, crawl under the heavy wooden crossbeams to investigate. It is damp and dark under the bridge, and although it takes some time for my eyes to adjust, I grope my way towards the strange locking breaths that seem to emanate from a fringe of rushes along the bank. I lean down and there, lying on her side in the shadowy reeds, I find a small, pale she-dragon, sick and close to dying. Her eyes are closed and when I put my hand on her neck to feel for life, her armoured eyelids roll back to reveal startling orange slits. She looks at me for a moment, and then closes her eyes. There is the faintest discernible pulse.

I kneel down and wrap the dragon in the jacket of my suit, then with some difficulty carry her up the slope to the majestic Fairmont Hotel Macdonald in Edmonton.

•

Mythology bubbles up within me, and all about me. The dragon lies on the bed in my suite at the Fairmont. Her breath is so shallow as to be almost non-existent. Sometimes her breathing catches and stops and I think she has died and I panic and wring my hands, but then there is an odd clicking noise in her throat and her delicate respirations begin again. I have turned out the lights, as the brightness seemed to agitate her. A phone rings repeatedly in the room next door. I turn on the flashlight app on my iPhone and examine her – a little squamous Drakania – with intricate trace markings curling about her body. On the webbed back foot is a long bone spur used to poison her attackers. Her sexual organ is a neat blue-rimmed fold and the waxy skin on her belly under the light of the iPhone has an opaline sheen that is heartbreaking.

Everything is happening and has happened and will happen again. Everything that exists has always existed and will continue to exist. Memory is imagined; it is not real. Don't be ashamed of its need to create; it is the loveliest part of your heart. Myth is the true history. Don't let them tell you that there are no monsters. Don't let them make you feel stupid, just because you are happy to play down in the dark with your flashlight. The mystical world depends on you and your tolerance for the absurd. Be strong, my darling ones, and believe!

And you, too, I say to my dragon. *Be strong!* I say, and I cover her body with a thin blanket. *Be strong!* I say, and there in my underwear I press my ear to the dragon's slow-moving side and adhere to the distant argument of her breath.

After a time, in a low whisper, I address my wife, in the hope that she may hear, all those many miles across the sea.

Hang in there, I say to my wife. *Be strong*, I say. *You can do it. There are a million of us, all over the world, breathing like you tonight.*

Vancouver
British Columbia

That night, on stage at the Orpheum, I stood at the deep end.
It was Canada Day and I was a single screeching lung of lack.
My dragon had not survived the night. She had died.
I had sat there and listened to her last slow susurration,
Bubble like a song from the wound in her side.

And the name of the song was 'The Butcher Boy',
That I heard in 1999 at the South Bank, with my wife,
About a young man called Willie who went away,
And a white English rose who took her life.

•

Arise and leap! We must take the first step alone!
The Muses and the angels shared a cigarette and cried.
Behind the Orpheum I paced and phoned home.
They told me our gods would outlive us. They lied.

Ring! Ring! Said the phone and it rang and it rhymed.
Ring! Ring! Said the phone, there is nobody home.
Ring! Ring! Said the phone and it rhymed and it chimed.
Ring! Ring! We must take the first step on our own.

•

On the way out of Vancouver we pull the bus over on the
Interstate Bridge. I carry the dragon's corpse to the barrier
wrapped in a small embroidered blanket I took from the Shangri-
La Hotel. I lift the bundle over the barrier and drop the whole lot
down into the river below.

I stand there a moment watching the relentless movement of the
water, half expecting to see the bundle rise to the surface and
bob jauntily down the river. But it does not.

Instead, I hear a voice.

You know the Chinese do not consider the dragon to be an evil creature at all. The dragon is seen as a god, ruler of the waters. Worship the dragon and you will find prosperity and peace.

Yeah, well, the dragon is dead, I say sadly, and turn.

Leaning against the barrier of the bridge, stands the black girl. She is dressed in a white mini-skirt with a red maple-leaf design printed on it. I smile in recognition.

Canada Day, I say.

She returns the smile and puts one naked foot up on the rail.

I've seen you before, right? Louisville?

The girl nods and salutes.

Thought so, I say.

The flushed fingers of the morning sun reach across the river and enfold the girl, igniting her in a nimbus of unworldly light. She steps up onto the barrier and presses her body against the new day. I move closer to her and together we look out across the waking city.

Vancouver, eh? I say. *Hey, have you ever heard Procol Harum's live version of 'Conquistador'? It was recorded in Edmonton.*

The girl turns toward me, shaking the hair out of her eyes, and nods.

Yeah, she says. *Great drumming.*

Totally, I say.

I've heard everything, she says, enigmatically. *Everything.*

Oh yeah? Well, it's pretty fucking awesome, is all I can say. Shit like that is worth sticking around for.

I wait there a moment, mesmerised by the girl standing on the barrier of the bridge, one hand clutching the suspension cable, the other gesturing curiously across the city, as if commanding it to rise.

You take care, I say after a time, *I've got to go,* and I turn away and head back down the bridge. As I arrive at the bus, I look back, but the girl has gone.

I climb onto the bus, my morning's business done, and thank the band – this brotherhood of transients – for their patience, but they are encased in their own private thoughts and do not acknowledge me, and I nod to the driver and say *let's go* and he pulls out into the traffic and we continue wordlessly on our way.

•

Maybe it was Marty, because Marty loves music, or it could've been Warren, who very much understands the idea of 'occasion', or perhaps it was Jim, always ready with a strong gesture, or was it Conway, for reasons entirely of his own, or George, maybe, who was just trying to deconstruct the eerie flamenco-like introduction, or it might've been Barry, although Barry doesn't like a lot of noise in the morning; I can't really be sure, but at some point, *someone* put a song on the bus's sound system.

Why was this particular song chosen? Maybe it was in respect of Canada Day, or that we were about to cross the Canadian border back into the USA, or perhaps it was just that we all needed something to help us through the sombre events of the morning, I can't in all honesty say, but as the singer's lugubrious voice filled the cabin of the bus – he was from Montreal – all the lights came down and the world withdrew, and, for a while, each of us was bound, suddenly and inextricably, together – and it helped, and it healed, and picking at a thread on my jacket sleeve, I drifted.

•

In two years' time the boy standing frozen with fear on the bridge will be fourteen years old and he will walk the mile and a half to his friend's house, under a flat, expressionless sky, the harsh Australian sun bearing down on him.

He will feel like an insect trapped under a child's malicious magnifying glass; the sun so fierce that it burns away all shadows and secrets and ambiguities with its interrogatory light. There is no escaping it.

The friend's big sister will invite him into her bedroom, an annexed weatherboard shed attached to the main house. Pieces of faded material have been stapled over the windows, so that the room is darker and cooler.

Check this out, she will say.

She will hand the boy a record cover, and the boy will see the mad face of a laughing man, and big block letters that say *Songs of Love and Hate* and he'll know even before she puts the needle on the record that he has something of untold value in his hands.

I stepped into an avalanche. It covered up my soul,

Leonard Cohen will sing, and the boy will suddenly breathe, as if for the first time, and fall inside the laughing man's voice and hide.

The boy will grow older, and over time there will be other songs – not many – ten or maybe twenty in a lifespan, that stand apart from the rest of the music he will discover. He will realise as he grows older still, and crosses the Canadian border and drives down into Seattle, that not only are these songs holy or sacred, they are *hiding* songs – what the Aztec Indians call *carrion* songs – that deal exclusively in darkness, obfuscation, concealment and secrecy. He will realise that, for him, the purpose of these songs has been to shut off the sun, to draw a long shadow down and protect him from the corrosive glare of the world.

•

There are nine sons of the Dragon.

> The Chaofeng dragon that likes precipices.
> The Pulao dragon that likes to cry.
> The Qiuniu dragon that likes music.
> The Baxia dragon that likes to carry heavy objects.
> The Suanni dragon that likes to sit down.
> The Chiwen dragon that likes swallowing.
> The Bi'an dragon that likes litigation.
> The Bixi dragon that is fond of literature.
> The Yazi dragon that likes to kill.

Seattle
Washington

And so it was, we crossed the border, down to Seattle,
And on the fire escape of the Paramount, after the show,
I smoked and listened to the people leaving the theatre,
And closed my eyes and dreamed I was washed up

On a vast white stretch of your neck and when I bit
Into it, I hardened like a coastal shelf and you shrieked
Through the blood; shrieked and tore at me,
And asked me where I was from. I said –

We have come down from the mountains,
We have crossed borders and rivers and prairies,
We have stood silent before visions of great natural beauty,
We have marvelled at miracles of bold engineering,
We have travelled along vast multi-laned highways,
We have traversed suspension bridges and keeping
To the shadows, entered into the majestic cities
To be with you tonight.

We have seen all that we had loved and loathed
And all was inside us.

On the fire escape of the Paramount I wondered where you'd gone.
I thought I had sole ownership of your body. I was wrong.

I thought I had sole ownership of *my* body. I was also wrong.
On the fire escape of the Paramount, I wrote this song.

My brain is a bee
My head is a hive
I unfold like a flower
The beekeeper's wife

The flower is a gigantic
Oozing sump of pollen
My head-hive splits open
My bee-brain is swollen

My bee-brain is swarming
Getting wiser than wise
A busy bee gorging on
Other beekeeper's hives

Buzz! Screams the bee!
The wide world roars!
Beekeeper is spent
Stinger withdraws

I called the song 'The Beekeeper's Wife'. I think the song hints at growing anxiety about my wife not answering the phone.

It also puts forward the idea that we do not have sole ownership of our dreams and that it is our right as artists to breathe freely and deeply the oxygen of ideas that engulfs the world, and to generally buzz around.

All that aside, the song is no good. It's dead-dragon dead. It's a hearse of verse. It's the sort of song that gets written when there is nothing to write about. It has been squeezed out of a dry, constricted aperture like an intestinal worm. It even *looks* that way on the page – pale, anorexic and half digested. I tried to make the song oval in shape, like a beehive, but check it out; it's actually shaped like a turd.

It appears as a headless, amputated corpse might appear or a concrete pylon that has not yet evolved into a column of light.

Still, I love you, little shit-shaped, stillborn song! Leap into my bag of sick! Maybe Bryan Ferry can find some use for you.

·

When Bryan Ferry sung the desolate old English ballad 'The Butcher Boy' that afternoon at the South Bank Centre in London, he did so alone at the piano, with a hushed abandon that reduced me and my wife to tears.

Was it the unearthly performance of the song? Or was it the song's devastating lyric? Or was it a diabolic combination of the two? I cannot say, but something unaccountable and premonitory happened at that moment as if the very song took up residence inside us, possessed us, and the course of our lives together was changed forever.

And at that moment in time, alone at the piano, Bryan Ferry became a *true* god, dangerously bestowing destinies, with the most beautiful voice in the world.

·

From inside the sick bag I hear strange, dissonant chanting. I open the bag and discover a set of miniature deities, surrounded by their prostrated and adoring acolytes.

Oh dear, I say and I drown them all in an old galvanised water trough, outside the Cheesecake Factory on Pine Street.

Then through the darkened streets of downtown Seattle, I sing the ancient ballad of 'The Butcher Boy'.

In London town where I did dwell
A butcher boy I loved right well
He courted me my life away
And now with me, he will not stay

I went upstairs to go to bed
And calling to my mother said
Give me a chair 'till I sit down
And a pen and ink 'till I write down

At every word she dropped a tear
And at every line cried Willie dear —
Oh, what a foolish girl was I
To be led astray by a butcher boy

And on Interstate 5, on our way to Portland, I continued to sing,

He went upstairs and the door he broke
He found her hanging from a rope
He took his knife and he cut her down
And in her pocket, these words he found

Oh, make my grave large, wide and deep
Put a marble stone at my head and feet
And in the middle, a turtle dove
That the world may know that I died of love

Portland
Oregon

It's a road-poem slash horror-story – think *The Hitcher* meets the *Book of Psalms* meets John Berryman meets a bit of Indianismo meets *The Waste Land* meets *Cocksucker Blues* meets *Nosferatu* meets Marilyn Monroe, Jimi Hendrix and Janis Joplin and anyone else who has drowned in their own sick, meets *Planes, Trains and Automobiles* meets *The Curse of the Mummy* meets Deepak Chopra meets – I drone,

As I sit in the penthouse of the Nines Hotel in Portland on a conference call to London.

The Head of Marketing cuts in – *little white rubber dead dragon keyrings, decapitated celebrity heads on pencils, sick bag tote bags and retro stars-and-stripes T-shirts, with 'Call the stewardess for bag disposal' across the chest –*

meets Kanye West meets homespun American folk ballad meets *The Book of Judith* meets a bit of Greek mythology meets the SCUM Manifesto meets *A Shropshire Lad* meets rock 'n' roll memoir meets *Apocalypto*, meets TripAdvisor meets motivational manual meets –

We need to tease out the decapitation theme – says my editor. *Didn't Nero stab himself in the neck? And, of course, John the Baptist and fucking Jayne Mansfield, right? Didn't she, you know, um, when she crashed her convertible –*

No, actually that was blunt force trauma, says my googling assistant –

My publisher says – *We could hire nine strippers, dress them as Muses and have them run through the Frankfurt Book Fair plucking their lyres and passing out sick bags! –*

meets Bret Easton Ellis meets the Earl of Rochester meets *Japanese Death Poems* meets Frederick Seidel meets *Mulholland Drive* meets a bit of Chinese mythology meets PornHub meets Butler's *Lives of the Saints* meets *The Odyssey* –

My editor, again — *You know, Aeolus was Keeper of the Winds and he gave Odysseus a big fucking bag of wind to blow him back to Ithaca, you know, on a gentle west wind. Throw this in as a riff on the bag motif —*

How about one single book reading event at the Strand from inside a giant Delta sick bag!

Trademark infringement, says my manager, who has hopped on the line.

Fuck Delta then! We'll do our own fucking sick bags!

meets *Arabian Nights* meets *The Ancient Mariner* meets *Moby Dick* meets the *Ramayana* meets —

•

Tonight I wrote down this line in the alley
Behind the Arlene Schnitzer Concert Hall,
In Portland, Oregon,
Where I smoked and sat,
I slide my little songs out from under you
And I was very happy with that.

But where are you?

•

When my wife entered the room, she did not see me. She crossed the bedroom and stood at the tall open window, gazing down at the gardens below. The sinking sun set the windows on fire. She did not move in the orange light. When at last she turned to look at me, I drew a sudden breath, for she was as white and intricate as a snowflake. She sat on the edge of the bed and in a small, business-like voice said,

They are coming.

Who are coming? I asked.

All of them. They are closing in. They want to kill me.

Who wants to kill you?

All of them. They are getting nearer.

Her face seemed to disassemble in the granulated light, then re-assemble as she lay down on the bed. From where I was perched, my wife looked as if she had been dropped there, out of the sky.

Well, I said, *if the past don't get you, the fucking future sure will.*

I'm serious, she said.

I know you are.

I smiled and came down and sat next to her.

Hey, no one is coming. It's okay. I'm here.

She traced her fingers down the contours of my face.

Oh, baby, you're not here, she said. *You're not here at all.*

And she pulled the sheet over her head.

My packed bags sitting in the hall.

•

Ring! Ring! Said the phone as I reared up and dialled.
Ring! Ring! Said the phone in the Nines Hotel.
Ring! Ring! Said the obliterating train and it smiled,
As it spun down the tracks *ring! ringing!* its bell.

San Francisco
California

Then I arrived in San Francisco and got sick.
The air was full of gas and ridiculousness.
It was too much of Allen Ginsberg's Grape Nuts, maybe,
In that melancholy sick bag repository on Columbus Avenue,
Or maybe it was one too many haunted sick bag nights,
Or whatever killed the dragon I now got!
But I lay on my bed in my suite at the Ritz-Carlton Hotel,
Shallow-breathing the dragon's same slow susurration,
That the world may know I died of love.

Let the world know that I died of love,
And I called you across five thousand miles,
And remembered what the angels said,
We are with you but you must take the first step alone.
It is their work to guide us through the dark,
And in time transport us home.

Are you there, darling? Pick, pick, pick.
Pick up the receiver and press it to your seashell ear,
And let the rush of angel air demand of us
That we take the first step alone.

My voice is speaking to you through the communication system
Of the Ritz-Carlton Hotel on Nob Hill. I am in bed.
And I am not coming home. I am not coming home.
I am pulling the blue plastic sheet over my head.

•

The train thunders around the bend on the other side of the river.
The track ballast rattles and shakes. The boy looks down at the
dark water swirling below him. He sees the concrete pylon. He
sees the branches of the tree. He looks up. The train has a huge
yellow face like a sun. The boy thinks of running back down the
track. The boy thinks of leaping into the river. The boy finds he
can do neither and stands frozen on the tracks. His eyes fill with
tears. The obliterating train shrieks and rushes toward him.

The Nine Primary Bedevilments of Creativity are –

Procrastination through fear.
Procrastination through indecision.
Procrastination through perfectionism.
Procrastination through waiting for inspiration.
Procrastination through chaos and misadventure.
Procrastination through illness and tiredness.
Procrastination through raising a family.
Procrastination through superstition and religion.
Procrastination through madness and suicide.

The Nine Secondary Bedevilments of Creativity are –

Procrastination through the Internet working.
Procrastination through the Internet not working.
Procrastination through Twelve Step Programs.
Procrastination through therapy and self-help literature.
Procrastination through charity work and saving the planet.
Procrastination through education and research.
Procrastination through hobbies and outside interests.
Procrastination through addiction.
Procrastination through sex.

The Nine Tertiary Bedevilments of Creativity are –

Procrastination through HBO.
Procrastination through dying your hair.
Procrastination through making money.
Procrastination through not making money.
Procrastination through not having the right equipment.
Procrastination through personal hygiene.
Procrastination through shopping.
Procrastination through decorating your workspace.
Procrastination through making unnecessary lists.

The Nine Quaternary Bedevilments of Creativity are —

Procrastination through vampirism.
Procrastination through lobotomy.
Procrastination through manual amputation.
Procrastination through cannibalism.
Procrastination through bankruptcy and recession.
Procrastination through environmental collapse.
Procrastination through terrorist attack.
Procrastination through apocalypse.
Procrastination through decapitation.

•

The train has a screeching yellow face. The face is blankly nothing. The silver tracks vibrate furiously and are eaten by the train. The train eats the rattling track ballast. Behind the train is nothing — not space, not time, not memory, not love. The sun hammers down, burning everything away to blank. The whistle shrieks its head off. The nothing-train will eat the boy. The boy begins to scream for his mother and rears up, *huh*, *huh*, *huh*, in his hotel bed, running sweat and black hair dye and blanching ghosts and corroded dreams, crying —

Memory is love! Oh my God! Love is memory! Help us!

Who the fuck am I? I shout. *Fucking help us!* I scream.

Los Angeles
California

Eventually everybody took up residence inside me.

As I stand on the edge of the king-sized bed
At the Sunset Marquis in West Hollywood,
Like a small erect god,
My heart is tied to the tracks of a shrieking train.
To my left, a shadowy concrete pylon, to my right,
The lethal branches of a half-felled tree.
You lie naked and partially submerged
In the muddy water below, thumbing nonchalantly
Through a motivational manual.

Eventually everybody took up residence inside me.

I am a haunted house howling and wheezing with memory.
Beds shake and cupboard doors spring open unaided,
And chairs stack and restack themselves.
Jets of ectoplasm spurt through the air.
My intestines ring with the sound of clanking chains.

You put the book to one side and raise your gash in the air.
You moan and discharge a bolt of feral tension that snaps
Your arms and legs backwards, your hard ridged throat,
Stretching and splitting open and your thin black animal
Tongue undulating towards me through the orange light.
I say —

I have come down from the hills,
I have crossed mountains and rivers,
I have travelled great highways,
I have entered your moist and shadowy fortress,
To be with you tonight.

I am the vehicle you have chosen to step in and out of.

You are as white as a snowdrop in the morning sun.

I cast a giant shadow against the sky.

Like a miniature deity, I gaze into the brown water.

I slide my little songs out from under you,

I am a small god crawling around a giant world,

Becoming an engorged god crawling around a small world.

Unfold yourself, my darling one!

We are luminous leapers, all of us, here in this bed tonight.

Together we are making our tomorrows different.

Austin
Texas

I am in a steakhouse in Austin, reading an Aztec poem called 'The Artist' in an anthology of poetry of the Indian North Americas, called *Shaking the Pumpkin*, edited by the brilliant Jerome Rothenberg, which I wish I could say I bought from City Lights Books on Columbus Avenue, in San Francisco, but didn't.

> *The true artist: capable, practising, skilful,*
> *Draws out all from his heart,*
> *Works with delight, makes things with calm, with sagacity,*
> *Works like a true Toltec, composes his objects, etc...*
>
> *The carrion artist: works at random, sneers at people,*
> *Makes things opaque, brushes across the surface of things,*
> *Works without care, defrauds people, is a thief.*

(translation by Denise Levertov)

Look out, you fuckers! Here I come with my sick bag song!

Working at random – Hey! I'm on fucking tour!
Sneering at people – Out of my way, you accursed acolytes!
Making things opaque – All that dark, imagined sex!

Whaddaya expect?

Is a thief – Okay, you've got me there, you crafty Aztecs!

Roll my sacrificial head down your temple steps!
OMG! Hail the mighty Conquistador!
At night Fearsome Panther Warrior and Great Eagle Warrior
Sweep the blood and sick and sperm off the bar-room floor.

•

The true artist is the expansive dream!
The carrion artist is the contracting nightmare!
The true artist is in the present and of the present!
The carrion artist lives in memory and history!

•

It's Country time, and I'm keeping Austin weird!
On the next table a Homo antecessor female
In a sequined Stetson scoops the brains
Out of her husband's decapitated head. She eats his eyes.
By the way, this is more or less true. I nail myself
To a blackened brontosaurus rib with duck fat fries and chew,
Then across the room hear *Yabba Dabba fucking Do!*
As Fred bashes complaining shopaholic Wilma
With his bowling ball and leaves her battered body
Under Willie Nelson's statue. Keeping Austin weird!

•

I am a small being crawling around a prehistoric world!
I am a tiny Mungo Man with a giant Pleistocene ding-dong!

We are walking through the lobby of the W Hotel,
Into the lunatic end of a Texan hen night.
I'm singing and swinging my sick bag song.
Let the world know that I died of love.

But hark! All about us, forest-fold,
Clad in the creamy entreatments of their transparent slips,
Were two hundred long, lean, tanned Texan legs
That pedestalled the raucous klaxons of their sex.

And the band and I were little old Toulouse-Lautrecs,
Standing on tippy-toe but still not able to reach the bar.
Here, the Texan girls said, let us sit you on our knees,
And lifted us up like naughty Howdy Doodies.

A cranberry and soda with ice and a piece of lime, please,
My square, mechanical mouth clacking as I spoke,
While the women poured liquor down their headless necks,
And I fucked off for a think and a smoke.

·

The critic is the true voice of our destructive nature.
It is the town crier of our innermost beliefs.
It walks up and down our veins and nerves ringing its bell.
You are wasting your time. You are not good enough.

Step back, it says, to the little boy. *Step back!*
The concrete pylon will crush you!
The branches of the half-felled tree will embarrass you!
Step back, it says. *Step back!*

The critic's voice is nothing new. It is a living voice inside us,
A persecution-mantra we've heard countless times before,
I think to myself, as I return to the Texan hen party.

·

Hey! I'm back! And this is a forest I'm happy to get lost in!
I am sitting in the happy lap of the longest legs in Austin.
Hello! My name is Howdy Doody Lautrec,
Sawing into the vast stretches of your Texan neck
With my savage hinged jaw.

Hop in my sick bag! All you wild Texan girls!
Look out, Patti! Watch out, Bryan!
There are a hundred new she-sheriffs in your sick bag town.
I'm heading back down, gonna get me some.

New Orleans
Louisiana

Down, down to old drowned New Orleans,
Past the Live Oaks and the Crepe Myrtle,
To the brackish waters of Lake Pontchartrain.
In every love story you'll find a dragon slain.
Here I am, with my lance dripping milky blood.
I have committed such carnage to be with you, my dear.
Take the damn photo! I feel stupid standing here.
Of course I'll sign the inside of your Louisiana thigh.
I'll tattoo it with my oozing lance in dragon's blood.
Yes, please! I love your town! It's sick!
With the streets of the Lower Garden District,
Named after the nine Muses.
Listen! You can hear them voodooing their lyres and singing,

It cut the women's neck and throw the head down
We pick them. Pick! Pick! Pick!
It cut the women's neck and throw the head down
We pick them. Pick! Pick! Pick!

I'm sick of hearing Sick Bag Steve and Windex Pete
Rapping their fucking washboards on Bourbon Street.

Belief is the belief that keeps on believing, but still
I stick my doubting fingers in your nail-wound to be sure.
In the morning they sweep the sawdust from the bar-room floor,
Sweep it clean and out onto the street.

Can you hear me, Sick Bag Steve?
Can you hear me, Windex Pete?

Still your spoons and lay your rattling washboards down.
The Muses are all tucked up in bed asleep.
If you listen very carefully you will hear their final dying sound.
It cut the women's neck and throw the head down.

•

That night in the Sonesta on Bourbon Street,
The hours passed like funerals till the dreaded four.
The naked, tangled Muses did softly snore and one by one,
Rubbed their tired eyes to stir – as an awful, nasal drone,
Emanated from a radio next door.

Is that who I think it is? shuddered Calliope, in dread.
It's Bob Dylan, I said, *for sure.*
And with a groan the Muses hung their beset, collective head.
Stop me if you've heard this one before.

•

I stepped gently from my trailer into a ferocious storm.
It was 1998 at Glastonbury on muddy Worthy Farm.
The artists' trailers were arranged in a neat square,
That boxed in a vast flooded slough. Thunder crashed.
It was pure mythic Greek. You could drown a cow.

I saw through the veil of pelting rain,
A trailer door open on the other side of the bog,
And a hooded figure step out. He climbed into a little boat,
And with a bag of wind under his arm, blew himself
Across that ghastly moat.

Lost in the dark reaches of his hood,
The stranger decanted from his boat and stood
Before me, yet I recognised – in slow motion –
The beak, the squint and the fluffy chin.
And all the world ground to a halt
To accommodate this thought. *It's him.*

Then slowly, extending from his sleeve,
A cold, white, satin hand took mine.
Hey, I like what you do, he said to me.
I like what you do too, I replied. I nearly died.
Then his hand retracted up his sleeve,

And Bob Dylan turned and took his leave,
Disappearing back into the rain.

But wait, Calliope, my impatient Muse! The tale does not
end here!

I walked back inside my trailer on that peculiar day
Feeling suddenly *drained*. Drained of blood! *Of life!*
And weak! So emptied out I could fade away.

Which is basically what I did for three whole years.
A dull, paralysing torpor hung over me.
An occasional note plucked from a disconsolate piano.
The odd word scratched into my teary notebook,
Then scratched out again.
Each night I dreamed of that slow vampiric hand
Extending from its awful cuff!

Stop now! said Calliope, rising to her feet,
Let it go! You are completely enough!

Soon after I noticed, just in passing,
Bob Dylan released *Love and Theft*,
Which got an A+ rating in *The Village Voice*.
Bob was back on top!

Meanwhile, I released *Nocturama*, which was a flop.

•

In the Royal Sonesta on Bourbon Street, we closed our eyes,
As the morning woke and its tail began to wag,
And just before we all fell back to sleep to softly snore
Someone kindly turned the radio off next door.

Washington
D.C.

The nine daughter-Muses ruffle the waters of the Potomac
With their sleepy breathing and in the Ritz-Carlton, D.C.
I do my laundry list – six shirts, six shorts, six socks a pair,
And write you a song and leave it on your answer machine.

The Recruitment Officer

A man approaches you and wants to take your photograph.
It is a form of recruitment.
It resembles something like belonging so you accept.
You have grown to be owned and long to belong.
There is no safe place on this earth to sit or stand or lay down.
Sit down, he says. Stand up, he says. Lay down.

Years later a different man approaches you
And asks you to marry him.
In a way he is as adrift and disgraced as you. You wed.
You arrange all the photographs before him on the bed.

He puts his hand inside you and pulls out the photographer.
He pulls out the first husband, the red-headed boy from Japan,
The famous artist, the gangster, the blurred maybe-men,
The ghost-children, all your ownings, all your growings,
All your leavings.

He attaches them to a gold band and spins them out into the sky.
Saying, sit down. Saying, stand up. Saying, lay down.

But this is not the last you see of them, because sometimes
At night you sense them crawling up the wainscot and moving
across the panelled ceiling of your room.
You think they are coming for you.
You think they want to kill you.

Abuse Man, Japan Man, Painter Man, Gangster Man, Ghost Baby,
Blurred Man, Husband Man.
The recruitment officer shifts in the shadows.
Sit down, he says. Stand up, he says. Lay down.

By the way, I never actually walked across the Big Four Pedestrian and Bicycle Bridge in Louisville, Kentucky, eating fried chicken. Warren, my violinist, did. He told me about it over a bowl of Grape Nuts in the breakfast room of the 21c Museum Hotel the next morning. It is what I call a *liberated* memory, appropriated but kept safe, lest we all forget.

•

I like 'The Recruitment Officer' a lot more than 'The Beekeeper's Wife', and with a bit of editing it could be pretty good. Having said that, I am a little disappointed with the passive victim role of my wife in the song and the hoary old idea of the husband-as-saviour-as-abuser. We deserve better from those overflowing fonts of inspiration, the nine Muses, daughters of Zeus and Mnemosyne! Neither of these roles even remotely corresponds to the way my wife and I conduct our lives.

I just wish she would pick up the fucking telephone.

Philadelphia
Pennsylvania

Fuck Rocky Balboa and his seventy-two stone steps to the top
Of the Philadelphia Museum of Art on Benjamin Franklin Parkway!
I climbed fifty and had to go back and begin again from the start.
Biggest Duchamp collection in the USA, mumbles Willner
From the back of the car as we take the divine Belmont,
Through West Philly to the Mann Center at Fairmount Park.
I was a nude descending a staircase in a pair of boxing trunks,
Into the anticipating dark. Ratso says that Sylvester Stallone
Wrote the screenplay for *Rocky* in three weeks flat.
Belief is the belief that keeps on believing.
And inspiration is the gift that brings and brings.
Here come the angels, descending golden staircases
Into Hollywood, with their script ideas tucked under their wings.
But the angels insist that we take the first step alone.
Everyone loves a good boxing story, especially God.
An underdog fighter beats the shit out of Apollo Creed,
The champion of the world. In *Rocky IV,* in the fifteenth round,
Old Rocky brings Russia to its heavyweight knees.
Over the Ukraine today they are pick, pick, picking
Airplane passengers out of the trees,
And as the lights come on, the band begins to play.
God punches the air! He cares!
I step into the light. I kneel at your altar. My severed head
Bounces down seventy-two stroboscopic stairs.

•

At the Mann Center at Fairmount Park, the audience are a rolling
river of hands, and after the show, in the dressing room, I pick at
a thread in my jacket sleeve, pick, pick, pick, then drift out into
the parking lot behind the auditorium for a smoke, where I sign a
young woman's thigh with a red marker, while backstage someone
delivers a pyramid of foil-wrapped Philly cheese steaks, but
starving Ratso checks his Urbanspoon app to find a place where
we could all sit down and eat, whereupon we drive around Philly,
unsuccessfully, for hours, looking for the restaurant, which we
eventually find, but the guy is mopping out, so we head back to

the Ritz-Carlton and sit on the massive columned steps and a bunch of us drink and smoke and laugh and eat bar food, and Willner quietly tells me that his friend Lou Reed clung hungrily to life, hungrily, but then calmly took his leave. More people show up after that and we all talk till late, and that night, in my hotel room, I pick at the unravelling thread in my sleeve and remember that the audience were like a rolling river of hands and the next morning housekeeping deliver my dry-cleaning to my room and I cry with happiness to find the laundered socks have come back secured with paper bands.

New York City
New York

There are those who work so they can stop.
Stopping is the *why* of work.
There are those who stop so they can work.
Working is the *why* of work.

•

I lie on my bed, in the Bowery Hotel, New York City
My Muse's decollated head, nestled in my lap,
Going lap, lap, lap, while I think of Sharon Olds,
Who wrote the best fellatio poems ever put to the page.
She writes lots of other great things as well.
Leonard Cohen had a shot in 'Chelsea Hotel' and of course,
Lou's 'Sister Ray' and Auden's porn-yawn, 'The Platonic Blow',
But none comes close to the dazzling Sharon Olds.
This is how the night unfolds. I peer through the crack
In Sharon Olds' closet with my sick bag song ready to blow.
I could only say that it was nice and I told my Muse so.

•

Later, I throw my Bowery window wide.
Up in the far right corner of the sky,
A rain cloud shaped like Elvis' severed head,
Cries its salt. And all across New York City
It pours beaded curtains of dewdrop jewels,
And rivers of ordinary love songs wash down
The gutters and fill the birdbaths and fountains
And the swimming pools. And from the bar below,
Nina Simone pounds the elephant ivory,
The Canadian maple and the strangling wire,
While up and down the hotel halls, the singing skeleton
Of Karen Carpenter glides and calls.
And as Roy Orbison deeply mines for cut diamonds
Of sorrowed sound, we begin to see a ghastly pattern!
Karen Dalton dangles from the rings of Saturn.
Hank Williams tilts to the side in the back

Of a powder-blue Cadillac, and Lou Reed's face
Appears on a napkin in a bar in Lower Manhattan.

Let the world know they worked to the end with love.
For there are those, poor things, who never start.
Let the world know they knew the *why* of goodbye,
That in love we often must depart.

Yes, in love we often must depart.
We will drown, poor things, in tears tonight,
But I've got to get an early start,
To Detroit on a Delta flight.

Detroit
Michigan

In Detroit Metropolitan Wayne County Airport,
A great wind blew apart the storage room that held
The Delta Air Lines sick bag supply. This is true.
And borne up by that great wind, they flew,
Those thousands of sick bags,
Like a host of paper-winged angels,
Over the breathtaking, bankrupt inner city of Detroit.

Please, do not forget me!
Pleaded the deserted megalopolis by the river.

We are the winged emissaries of God!
Do not despair! You will not be forgotten!
In time, everyone will take up residence inside you.

Please, do not forget me!
Implored the fugitive man, hiding in the hotel.

We are the winged emissaries of God!
Prepare yourself! We will not forget you!
We have come to bear you back home.

Please, do not forget me!
Cried the shivering boy on the train tracks.

We are the winged emissaries of God!
Do not fear! You will not be forgotten! Listen!

You will stand on the edge and think you are alone,
But you are not alone.
All history is fixed to your ankle, all memory,
All family and friends, all enemies,
All politicians and decision-makers,
All businesspersons,
All masters and teachers –
They will hang like grand pianos from your heels,
But slow your breath, and with boldness take the first step.

Fall over the precipice with the whole world weighted on,
And you will see.
You will soar on your brave sick bag wings!
It will be difficult but you will rise!
But be warned! You will be judged and judged harshly,
But only by those who dared not leap.
They will sit around and say, *that traitor*, that *fucking poser*,
Look at him! Who does he fucking think he is?

But you are none of these things.
You are a beautiful leaper,
Trailing ribbons of joy and gratitude
Around a limitless sun.

•

In the car park outside the Masonic Temple, I smoke with my
hatless driver, and later drive aimlessly around the city, and
later still, stand on the Ambassador Bridge and watch the
setting sun ignite the majestic and indifferent river.

A familiar voice says,

*The Grosse Point billionaire 'Matty' Moroun owns this bridge. It is
the only privately owned border crossing between the United States and
Canada. Even so it cost the fucking taxpayer hundreds of millions of
dollars. But the view from up here at night is awesome!*

The black girl in the stars-and-stripes mini-skirt smiles at me
and puts her foot on the barrier, her toes curling around the rail.
I notice she has two maple leaves, like red handprints, stencilled
on the back of her skirt.

You again, I say. *What are you doing?*

I'm flying, she says. *Wanna come?*

I stare down at the dark, muddy water below.

I said, *You're not flying, you're falling. There is a subtle difference in outcome.*

Oh yeah? And what do you think you are doing?

I look down at the city again. From here the city resembles a severed head, incinerated and discarded by the side of the river; its cavernous eye sockets are empty, bundles of dead nerves dangle from its neck, its shattered mouth gapes, a few desolate wires hang from its stark, scorched skull and, suddenly and incomprehensibly and so foreign to my body I could weep, I feel my heart expand with what I can only describe as a sensation of *hope*. Is there a word for that? Hope in the face of great calamity?

What am I doing? I don't know, I say. *Stalling, I guess.*

Sounds about right, she says.

I am working though, I reply.

The girl laughs and says, *Yeah, right.*

The girl stands up on the rail, the muscles in her brown legs contracting beneath her skirt that now flaps like a flag in the wind. The lights of the bridge loop through the night sky above her. She holds onto the girder and presses her young body into the wind.

It's so fucking beautiful up here!

You're telling me, I say and turn away. I'm crying now.

See you later, I say. *Take care.*

I start to walk back down the bridge to where the black SUV sits idling. My driver is a dark shadow in the front seat. I wipe my streaming eyes with my sleeve. The girl, balanced so perilously on the barrier that she appears to be dancing, calls out to me, across the night.

Hey you! It's probably time you went home, don't you think? Isn't there someone waiting for you? That's the true and righteous work, right there! How about it? You know! Suck it in and take the leap!

Then in the blink of an eye she is gone.

•

The Delta Air Lines sick bag helpfully instructs:
'Call the stewardess for bag disposal.'
The Sick Bag Song is full of all that I love and loathe,
And all is inside myself. It is so full now it's gonna burst!
Call the stewardess for bag disposal!
Then I can begin again and tomorrow leap differently!

Ding! Dong! I alert the stewardess to my need!
Ding! Dong! My sick bag is ready to blow!
Ding! Dong! The plane's chemotrail is a fucking scandal!
Ding! Dong! The stewardess has leapt from the plane!

Toronto
Ontario

The man who has just walked on stage at the Sony Centre in Toronto does not realise that he is not a man at all.

He is the dream of a boy standing on a shuddering railway track.

The man and the boy dream each other.

They remember each other.

The man reaches out and takes hold of the boy and, hand in hand, they step into the spotlight. They walk themselves to the world's edge. The engine of sound is deafening. The earth shudders beneath their feet. They look down into the cosmic depths below.

•

We have traversed borders.

We have passed through regenerated inner cities, through inner cities in the process of regeneration, and dying inner cities.

We have moved across the land, over wheat fields, mustard fields, corn fields, bean fields and fields of sunflowers.

We have travelled along great free-flowing bodies of water – the Cumberland, the Ohio, the confluence of the Kansas and Missouri Rivers, the Milwaukee, the St Croix, the Mississippi, the South Platte, the Elbow and the Bow, the Saskatchewan, the Fraser, the Duwamish, the Willamette, the San Francisco, the Los Angeles, the Colorado, the Potomac, the Schuylkill, the Hudson, the Detroit, the Delaware, the Don and the St Lawrence Rivers.

We have become lost in cities of great architectural beauty. We have kept to the shadows and at night allowed ourselves to be seen. We have looked out and marvelled at distant skylines.

We have communed in masonic temples, public parks, 700-acre farms, destination theatres, Spanish Baroque style theatres, French and Italian Baroque style theatres, Italian Renaissance style theatres and theatres in the Spanish Gothic style. We have communed in Neoclassical style theatres made out of Alabama limestone, theatres in the Renaissance Revival style, vaudeville theatres, movie palaces renovated into multiplexes, performing arts, culture and community facilities, Unification churches, concert halls in the Moorish Revival style and vast open-air auditoriums.

We have driven thousands of miles in buses, vans, cabs, limousines and suburban utility vehicles. We have ridden trains, trams and trolley cars. We have walked down teeming peopled streets and streets empty of people.

We have flown through the sky on British Airways, Delta Air Lines, Air Canada, Alaska Airlines, United Airlines, American Airlines, Southwest Airlines and sat at the departure lounges of Minneapolis-St Paul International Airport, Denver International Airport, Edmonton International Airport, Portland International Airport, San Francisco International Airport, LAX, Austin-Bergstrom International Airport, Louis Armstrong New Orleans International Airport, JFK and the Toronto Pearson International Airport.

Our food has come from artisan bakers, organic butchers, fish mongers, fast food outlets,˙ taco stands, chicken shacks, salad bars, sushi conveyor belts, pizza boxes, all-night diners, five-star restaurants, road stops, food courts, farmers' markets, in-house catering, minibars, hotel breakfast rooms, coffee franchises, delicatessens, restaurants, bars, burger joints and hotdog vendors. We have received room service.

We have sat in domed lobbies, designed after the Pantheon in Rome and built from 700 tons of pink marble. We have sat backstage in rank and desolate dressing rooms.

We have visited television studios and radio stations without any recollection of doing so.

We have lain in a bed in the Sheraton Hotel, Nashville, and stared at the ceiling. We have gazed in the mirror of a bathroom in the InterContinental Hotel, Kansas City, and we have vomited shellfish in a toilet bowl in the Grand Hotel in Minneapolis. We have written out our dry-cleaning lists in the Edmonton Fairmont Hotel Macdonald and the Ritz-Carlton, Washington. We have masturbated in the Bowery Hotel in New York City and the Sunset Marquis in West Hollywood. We have sat in the rose garden in the Ritz-Carlton in San Francisco and chain-smoked. We have been propositioned in the lobby of the W Hotel, Austin. We have watched all-night TV in the Four Seasons in Denver. We have been manicured in the spa at the Shangri-La in Vancouver. We have watched PornHub in 21c Museum Hotel, Louisville, and also the Nines in Portland. We have stolen the bathrobes from the Ritz-Carlton, Philadelphia. We have won large amounts of money at the casino in the MGM Grand Hotel in Detroit and we have ridden the elevators to the penthouse of the Trump in Toronto.

We have been tended to by concierges, bellboys, Asian maids, Hispanic maids, African-American maids and maids of indeterminate ethnic origin, uniformed doormen, dry-cleaning services, turn-down artists, dentists, doctors, hypnotists, homeopaths, pharmacists, drug dealers, lawyers, agents, shake-down artists, barmen, waitresses, fry cooks, Michelin chefs, receptionists, managers, personal assistants, assistants to personal assistants, assistants to assistants to personal assistants, publicists, promoters, production managers, insurance brokers, accountants, marketing managers, make-up artists, hairdressers, photographers, cameramen, security guards, bodyguards, non-uniformed doormen, travel agents, pilots, co-pilots, air hostesses, ground staff, luggage handlers, lift drivers, bus drivers, cab drivers, limo drivers, squeegee merchants, drum technicians, guitar technicians, road crews, side-of-stage guys, monitor engineers, front-of-house guys, lighting guys, merchandising guys, road managers and assistant road managers, all to be here with you –

North America, tonight!

We are responding to your vibrations as they electrify the tracks.

•

In Nashville,
You were the accelerated rhythm of a small boy's heart.

In Manchester,
You were a blue plastic sheet that hid a headless corpse.

In Louisville,
You were a black hummingbird on a suspension bridge.

In Kansas City,
You were a pile of bison skulls waiting to be ground into fertiliser.

In Milwaukee,
You were an inky, screaming reflection trapped in a hotel mirror.

In Minneapolis,
You were a concrete pylon turning into a glorious column of light.

In Denver,
You were the entrails of a dismantled walkie-talkie.

In Calgary,
You were a cake of pine sap trapped in a block of ice.

In Edmonton,
You were a white she-dragon drawing her last loving breath.

In Vancouver,
You were the demented face of a laughing poet.

In Seattle,
You were a miniature Shiva floating in a galvanised water trough.

In Portland,
You were a sun-faced train thundering along the tracks.

In San Francisco,
You were a drugstore beetle in a bowl of Ginsberg's Grape Nuts.

In Los Angeles,
You were a gloop of ectoplasm spurting through the orange air.

In Austin,
You were a Texan girl's honeysuckle, dewdrop sex.

In New Orleans,
You were Windex Pete's battered gravestone washboard.

In Washington,
You were a valued item of misplaced laundry.

In Philadelphia,
You were the autographed inner thigh of a glum teenager.

In New York,
You were a man vomiting snowdrops into an airline sick bag.

In Detroit,
You were an ejaculating water feature in Wayne County Airport.

In Toronto, here, right now, each of you are changing form.
You are becoming the mother of the nine Muses, Mnemosyne.
Mnemosyne means memory. You are becoming memory.
Please remember me. Please do not forget me. Please.

And in Montreal, tomorrow, come, all of you
And you will see a small and vanishing god,
Lying in shattered pieces, by a moonlit lake.
You will be the remembering moon.
You will be the remembering lake.
So, until then –

·

The man who is walking on stage at the Sony Centre in Toronto
does not realise that he is not a man at all.

He is the dream of a boy, with tears in his eyes, standing frozen
on a shuddering railway track.

The man and the boy dream each other.

They remember each other.

The man approaches the boy and reaches towards him.

Hand in hand, they turn and step into the roaring light.

The sound of the faceless, shrieking train is deafening.

They walk themselves slowly to the world's edge.

The ground beneath them shudders and quakes.

Each understands that the other may be forgotten.

Each understands that the other may die.

The universe holds its breath.

•

Together and alone, they leap.

Montreal
Québec

Outside the old Hotel St Paul,
The band all hug and say goodbye,
Then I make my way to Lake Montreal,
And beneath a wood of silver maple trees,
I watch a glow rise off the lake,
As the night begins to fall.

And by that luminescent lake,
And under the silver maple trees,
I give my sick bag a gentle shake,
And all those awful, raging hearts fall out.
And one by one they run away,
I dial you on my phone.

And as the moon lies down upon the lake,
I sit upon the forest floor,
And under the silver maple trees,
I know in truth we are not alone,
Then I fold my sick bag into four,
Ring. Ring. Click. *Hello?*

•

I am coming home.

Nick Cave, 2014

The Nine Ways of Undying Gratitude

Thanks to my mother
Thanks to the band
Thanks to the crew
Thanks to the audience
Thanks to the management
Thanks to the publishers
Thanks to the cinephiles
Thanks to the butcher
Thanks to my wife for all